LIONESS CHANT

By Fyna & Nefertiti

Foreword by Makeda Coaston

Lioness Chant

First published by Karia Press in 1989

Copyright © Fyna Dowe and Nefertiti Gayle, 1989

Illustrations by Fyna Dowe

Front cover illustration by Fyna Dowe

Typesetting and Design by Karia
Printed and bound in Great Britain by
Biddles Ltd, Guildford and King's Lynn

ISBN 0 946918 44 9

Karia Press
41 Rheola Close
London N17 9TR
United Kingdom

Contents

Foreword

There are a lot of attitudes towards women which limit their authority and power. A lot of myths that are gratefully finding their deaths: "Woman — you chat too much"; "Be seen and not heard"; "Be a silent worker and suppporter" — not a vocal leader or inovator. They go on and on, these epitaphs of a woman's right to be spontaneous, outrageous and courageous.

There have always been women who refuse to shut up and submit to an unjust cause. Rebel women, wariors, sustainers of families and builders of institutions. LIONESS CHANT emerged from this tradition. As creative messengers, Nefertiti Gayle and Fyna Dowe combine poetry and music which carry both bite and humour.

For four years LIONESS CHANT have appeared throughout Britain and France. They have quickly gained a reputation as incisive witnesses of struggle. Provocative and commanding in delivery they are best known for an earthy wit that unleashes a frontal attack on issues threatening African cultural survival.

This premiere publication also includes work not usually presented that show the '-CHANT' as more vulnerable and introspective.

Although in the early stages of their creative growth, LIONESS CHANT continue to experiment with form and focus. This collection documents that process and holds a process for much more to come.

Makeda Coaston, 1987.

Sold Subject to Contract

Sold subject to contract
Sold subject to contract
Sold subject to contract — Debeers!
Sold subject to contract — Sherwoods!
Sold subject to contract — Cape!
Sold subject to contract — B.P.!
Sold subject to contract — Delmonte!
sold subject to contract — Tesco!
Sold subject to contract — Barclays!
And all the other banks of the West
— And their partners in crime.

Train a coming! Train a coming!
Get your papers here!
Times! Young Socialists! *Morning Star! Mail! Guardian!*
Free Mandela, Free Mandela!!
Free Mandela, Free Mandela!!
Get your papers here!

But what about those on Roben Island?
    what about those in the shanty towns
    what about those in the home of whites?
What about the youth dem a fight?
— Dem a fight! Dem a fight!

Demonstration this Saturday — all night vidual!
Picket! Picket! Picket!

Free Mandela! Winnie Mandela!
Free Mandela! Winnie Mandela!
Free Mandela! Winnie Mandela!

But what about those on Roben Island?
What about those in the shanty towns?
What about those in the home of whites?
What about the youth dem a fight?
— Dem a fight! Dem a fight.

You right! You right! You right!
It's not just Mandela!
Boy dem really making money
Out a we suffering.
It's not just Mandela.
Oppressors feeding on human flesh
Now that is their thing.
They a carry the swing.

Train a coming! Train a coming!
Free Mandela! Free Mandela! Free Mandela!

But what about those on Roben Island?
What about those in the shanty towns?
What about those in the home of whites?
What about the youth dem a fight?
— Dem a fight! Dem a fight.
What about those Blacks who kill their own
Blacks set up by investors
To fight dem own Black???

Blood run from children body.
Oppressors eat
And fill up dem belly belly sweet.
Trading in human meat.

Sold subject to contract.
Sold subject to contract.
Sold subject to contract.

How many Jews whose foreparents
Were killed in the gas chambers
— Now invest in South Africa!

How many Indians whose foreparents
Were murdered by the British
— Now invest in South Africa!
And Russia
Stretching out invisible hands
Over the African land
With a perfect socialist plan.
— Now invest in South Africa!

The Japanees
who were brought to their knees.
When the Americans dropped the Bomb
On Hiroshima and Nagasaki
— Now invest in South Africa!

How many British, American,
And all the other
Europeans who pussy-foot around
And fart-ass-around in the United Nations
On issues dealing with Sanctions,
Exploitation
— And dehumanisation of peoples.
— Now invest in South Africa!

And how many of us Africans
That is YOU, and me
— People of the Caribbean, America, Europe

Asia and Australasia
— Now invest in South Africa!

That is You! You! You! and You!! . . .
Stop murdering you brother!
Stop murdering your sister! . . .
Stop invest in South Africa!! . . .

Aids

First starvation then Herpes,
Now another deadly disease.

Yak! Yak! What is that,
It ain't grandma's pussy cat.

Aids, Aids, don't come in *grades*,
Don't come in *shades*,
And it never *fades*.

Watch out, Watch out!
There's panic about,
Some say you can catch it from the mouth,
Beware if you must sleep about.

Aids, Aids, don't come in grades,
Don't come in shades,
And it never fades.

Some people try to say it is us,
Spreading all this Aids stuff,
This is a political situation,
It concerns every nation.
We are here to show the truth,
And make it plain to all of you.
That what we really need to know is:
Where did Aids start to grow?

Aids, Aids, don't come in *grades,*
Don't come in *Shades,*
And it never *Fades.*

What about those with Sickle Cell Anaemia?
And those who have Haemophilia?
Now they're all going mad!
Because they don't know,
Whose blood they've had?

Aids, Aids, don't come in *Grades,*
Don't come in *Shades,*
And it never *Fades.*

Takes four years to incubate!
Some sit in fear and wait
Some sit and masturbate!
What people have to do is,
Not to catch aids like the flu,
Acquired immune deficiency syndrome,
Don't let in your home.

Aids, Aids don't come in *Grades,*
Don't come in *Shades,*
And it never Fades, Fades, Fades.

© Fyna Dowe/Nefertiti Gayle

Summer Time

Summer time and the living is easy.
Bricks are flying,
And the flame is high.
Your daddy's rich,
Cos he's a capitalist.
So hush down pressor
We're gonna make you cry.

Summer time and the living is still easy,
Bobylan a come to commit their crime.
Plastic bullets, C.S. gas and water cannon,
To try and cool the vibes.

But this summer time,
The living won't be easy.
Cos we'll be watching you by and by,
And any time you commit your crime,
We're gonna make you down pressor cry and
cry.

Don't say how don't say maybe
We're gonna make you cry.
Don't say how don't say maybe
We're gonna make you cry.

13

Racist Today

Forward home to Africa,
We're coming home to Africa,

Racist today, go away,
We don't want you in our way,
Racist today, go away,
We don't want you in our way.

Tek you han off we land,
Tek you han off we land.

Get off we land,
Come off we land.
Get of we land,
Come off we land.

Stop teef we diamond,
Stop teef we gold,
Leave we minerals alone.

Stop teef we copper,
Stop teef we oil,
Leave we Uranium alone.

Get off we land western man,
Get off we land western man,
Stop come with you nuclear plan.

Multinationalist get off we land,
Imperialist get off we land,
Communist get off we land.
Leave we people alone.

Racist today go away,
We don't want you in our way!
Racist today go away,
We don't want you in our way!

Tek you han off we land,
Come of we land,
Get off we land,
Step off we land.

Stop invest, stop mek trests, stop infect.
Africa is our land,
There forever we shall stand.
Africa is our home,
There forever we shall roam.

© Fyna Dowe/Nefertiti Gayle

We Are Not
This Feminists

We are not this feminist . . ist, ist,
We are not into this business,
We are not into this business.

No boder shake you head,
wid you trendy spread,
Say you no check a man,
Where you come from.
You not into positiveness,
Only this kind of feminism your request.
We are not this feminist . . ist . . .ist,
We are not into this business,
We are not into this business.

African women from time,
Have been working on the front line,
Struggling with her man,
To keep a firm han.
Daughters have to be firm,
An in time they will learn,
If de man is de oppressor,
An him put her under pressure.
Den she ha fe manners her man,
An mek him know where she stand.

We are not this feminist . . ist . . ist,
We are not in this business,
We are not into this business.

Feminism they say is the issue,
But his they misconstrue.
How can a African woman be this
    kind of feminist,
When her people suffer social
    and racial injustic!

We have to rebuild our family,
For the sake of our humanity,
Feminism in this place and time,
Is following another line,
Tradition and culture must be bold,
As political lies begin to unfold,
This kind of feminism,
Don't deal with us,
It stems from,
Insecurity and mistrust.

We are not this feminist . . ist . . ist,
We are not into this business,
We are not into this business.

It does not have to be a physical situation,
To determine a man an woman relation,
Jus nuff discipline and self control,
Working together towards the same goal.

No woman must work till she drop,
A man must also scrub a pot,
Change him pickne nappy,
And keep him pickne happy.

We are not this feminist . . ist . . ist
We are not this feminist . . ist . . ist.

© Lioness Chant 1985

17

We Have Come

It's time to change,
Re-arrange the set,
We have come to collect,
Our long over due debt.
No credit!
You've had it far too long,
And the hire-purchase agreement,
Has gone wrong!

So we come to collect,
What is rightfully ours,
And the interest that is owed.
If you don't pay up in full,
We will? Tread on your toes.
Just like you did,
When you took our land.
Just like you did,
A Bible, gun in your hands.
Just like you did,
When you herded us on ships,
To make that long never ending trip.

We have come, for what is now due,
We have come and we want our land too,
We have come,
But we will never ever stoop as low as you,
We have come!
We have come!
We have come!
We . . . Have come!

© Fyna Dowe 1984

18

Mint Tea As
A Prefrance

Me say me want,
A cuppa mint tea.
Me jus want,
A cuppa mint tea.
Me say circe tea,
It bitter like hell.
An chalklate tea,
Mek you belly swell.
An de one ginger root,
It will bun you as well.
Me jus want a cuppa mint tea.

Me no need fever grass,
Me na get sick.
Me no wan no cinamon stick,
An boil orange peel,
Me no care fe it,
Me jus want a cuppa mint tea.

© Nefertiti Gayle

Is It Just A Natural Thing?

Everybody knows,
The sun shines from the sky,
And the rain beats down to the ground,
From on high,
That is just a natural thing, But,
That is just a natural thing, But;

When people are suppressing people,
Is it just a natural thing?
When people are denying people,
Is it just a natural thing!?
Is it just a natural thing!?

Some say: The earth spins round and round,
And that gravity is the thing,
That holds us to the ground.
And that is just a natural thing,
And that is just the nature of thing, But,

When people are mis-informing people,
Is it just a natural thing?
When people are destroying people,
For no reason,
Tell me . . . Is it just a natural thing?
        Is it just the nature of things?
        Is it just a natural thing?

Party Afe Party

Me na go a people party
Fe hole up de wall
People shouldn't go a people party
An stan up an stall.

Party afe party
No fe lean gainst people wall.

Party afe party
No fe stan up
Like you
Ready fe fall.

Me na pay me big dunsi
Fe go to a dance
Fe cut eye cut eye
An stan up inna trance
People go to a dance
And spend dem big money
Dress up on de 99
Sweet as honey.

Some in peacock feather
Some in suede an leather.

Cris/Cris ganze
Beaver hat
Gwan like dem cool
Stan up like dem fool.

Gold drip from dem neck
Dem face look vex
Like dem ready fe mek
Big threat.

Me na go to a show
An not appreciate the band
Generate vibration
An try stimulate
Dem creation
People go to a show
And sit in front row
Look up
Push-up dem mout
and when de band shout
De mout still push-out.

Me na go to a party
Fe go de an fight.
When me get high
Me a enjoy de night.
People go to party
Fe go de an fight
And when dem get high
Dem can't last de night
Some go de out a frustration
Some go de out a spite
Some go de because dem
Feeling up-tight.

When you go to a party
You fe enjoy you self
Else stay inna you yard
And fix you kitchen shelf.

No go to a party and
Start bodderation
Jus go de man an
Raise vibration.

© Nefertiti Gayle

Mental Enslavement

Mental enslavement,
Characteristic down gradement.
Continual enslavement.
Control, no maintenance.
Are the politics of the West,
At their hypocritical best.

Some a dem a Black!
Some a dem a white!
Some a dem a Black and white.

Traitors,
Agents,
All wanting to control,
The plight,
Of African life.

An their intentions,
Is to wipe us out.
Control our minds
Feed us with so called equality.
Divide us up,
Shut us up,
Giving some of our countries,
Loans,
Negotiating with our Fascist leaders
By phone.

And the puppets,
Sell us out,
They perform to the people,
Wid dem mouth,
The informers inform,
They perform to hide their shame.

An we blame,
Each other,
For the pain,
When we all should release,
The chains on our brains.

For the rape,
Of our race,
Is still going on,
And we have to stop,
The rape,
Which the West,
Tries to prolong,
On An An On
  An On An On
    An On An On

© Nefertiti Gayle

We A Bubble
We A Bubble

We a bubble on de line,
Everything look fine,
Some a we a go,
Out o'we blasted mind,
We a bubble.
Volcano jus a rubble,
An we ina trouble,
All nation ina trouble.

Middle Eas' war gone real far,
Iraqi planes bombing again.
Oil on the brains,
Running through Reagans veins!
We a bubble,
We a bubble bubble.

Iranian planes bombing again,
Lebanon in trouble,
P.L.O. on de double.

Israelie war stretch real far,
Right down ina South Africa.
Part of a global mafia.
We a bubble,
We a bubble bubble.

We a bubble on de line,
Everything look fine,
Some a we a go,
Out o'we blasted mind,
We a bubble.
Volcano jus a rubble,
An we ina trouble,
All nation ina trouble.

Pan European putting on the heat,
Wanting all we Africans,
To bow down at their feet.
We a bubble,
We a bubble bubble.

Botha a come,
To put us to sleep,
Reagan a come,
To step on we feet,
Thatcher a come,
To kick we underneath,
Mitterand a come,
To see if we weep,
And when you think,
De have us at we feet,
Russia a come,
To make we deplete,
We a bubble,
We a bubble bubble.

Buff!
We a come with the warrior beat!
We ha' fe fight this mental sleep!
Stan firm on we own two feet!

We a bubble.
Our people ina trouble,
But dem na burst we bubble,
Cos we a go de on de double,
An put dem ina trouble.

We a bubble on de line,
Everything look fine,
Some a we a go,
Out o'we blasted mind,
We a bubble.
Volcano jus a rubble,
An we ina trouble,
All nation ina trouble.
All nation ina trouble . . . .
All nation ina trouble . . . .

I Remember

As far back as I can remember,
Was the age of three.
The palm trees,
Blue sea,
And the hanging coconuts,
From trees.

Having grapefruit in the yard,
With grandma,
And the boy next door who bothered me.
All these things happened,
At the age of three.

The night of mosquitoes,
Was strange to me.
They came,
And mother with all her virility,
Got rid of them,
Just for me.
But mother who I loved so dearly,
Beat me with a,
Bamboo stick,
Which she'd cut from a tree.
But the next day,
All was forgiven.
For mother had the biggest party,
You ever saw,

Just for me.
It was the boy next door,
That worried me.
He would tell me tales,
of little green men,
Who would,
Cut off my head,
And be ruthless to me.
All these things I remember at,
The age of three.

© Nefertiti Gayle

From Where I Am Looking

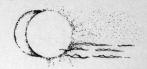

So I said I had ambition,
But was it the right thing to say?
From where I was looking.

I was determined to be strong,
Didn't care if it was wrong.
From where I was.

I gave them what they wanted,
Followed the golden rule.
Even some times playing clown,
Acting fool.

But, always, I kept my own mind,
I wasn't gong to leave that behind.

Tried everything,
I'd try anything once.
Remember . . . .
I remember,
To life there's a whole lot more,
From where I am looking.

Now,
With some of my mind still my own,
Searching for the rest,
In a place called home.
Is where I am looking,
Because I'm home . . . I am home.
Afrika!

© Fyna Dowe 1983

33

Daughter

Daughter,
No slaughter ya man,
No mek him go brok bank.

Style style,
You a par style,
Shoes from grants and panache,
Boots from ravels,
You like what Harrods have to sell.

You pap style,
An ya man unemployed,
Can't get no job.

All ya wan is fashion,
An ya man on material ration,
An you only intention,
Is to sport fashion.

So you want a carpet,
An you never did get it,
Cause sylvia have one,
An marcia goin get one.
Both of dem have,
A new shag pile,
An all you want is style.

Him promis you video,
An you never did get one,
An Claudette going get one,
De new V.H.S.

An all you want is style,
An de pickney put pressure,
Say dem want soda streema,
An mother say what happen,
To the new net curtains,
And de new fridge freezer,
Was de only reason why,
You never did throw him a street,
Fe babylon fe ketch him feet,
A walk street.

Daughter no go wild,
No pap style understand,
Western man plan to divide,
You an you African man.

© Nefertiti Gayle

Fry Up

Fry up, Fry up, Fry up,
    Fry up, Fry up, Fry up!
Dem a bun up!

What dat a burn?
We have fe learn,
Not burn,
Not perm, or stay sof-frooo . . .

Fry up, Fru up, Fry up,
    Fry up, Fry up, Fry up,
Dem a bun up!
Water perm,
Cream perm,
Jelly Cream,
Bleach face,
Straightened nose for smaller space.

Fry up, Fry up, Fry up,
    Fry up, Fry up, Fry up,
Dem a bun up!
An when you walk down de street,
An de rain come like sleet,
Is den you turn natty dread'
Oh dear! What's happened to my hair?

Fry up, Fry up, Fry up,
    Fry up, Fry up, Fry uo,
Dem a bun up!

A wa we shame of?
Dry head?
A wa we shame of?
Kinky head?
A wa we shame of?
Natty head?
An you turn round in fear,
Saying yes, yes, I'm aware,
But I want to straighten my hair.

We poroxide our minds,
Till alas we gone blind,
In the fire of destruction,
There is no retribution.

An still we go to the grave,
Full of Babylon pollution,
It's time we stop dying,
Having found no solution!

Fry up, Fry up, Fry up,
    Fry up, Fry up, Fry up,
Dem a bun up!
Dem a bun up!
Dem a bun up dem head,
Dem no like natty dread,
Dem only want straighten head,
Dem a bun dem a bun dem a bun up.

Mabinte/Fyna Dowe/Nefertiti Gayle

International Projection

It's international time honey,
That means stop accepting,
Conscience money.
It's international time honey,
That means stop being willing to accept,
What's said in a hurry.

It's international time honey,
That means stop being caught up,
In news and views,
Democratic acts?
Start to face the facts!

The fact is,
It's international time,
Time to check *you.*
Everything *you* think say and do.
Check *your* mind.
Make sure *you* have not left it behind.
Check the words *you* speak,
Let them be throughful — not weak!
Respect women,
Respect men,
Respect youth,
Because, in plain truth,
Together we must move hand in hand,
To regain our spiritual home land.

© Fyna Dowe 1983

I Sight a Dead Lady

I sight one dead lady,
In a crochous bag.
Laying in a gully beside a hog.
Last night me hear gun shot.

"Pow"

Me hear M.16 a lick,
An if you no careful
You get a beatin wid it.
So cool out ina you littl shack,
No bodder wonder by the gully track,
Before man an man go drapes,
You up an say,

"What you defen on dis side of de fence"

And before you even get a chance,
Fe hick up,
"Pow",
P N P corner,
J.L.P. on ya,
Deliverance a come.

Run out de cubans,
And bring in American guns,
Foreign exchange,
An more poverty and pains
Price sky high,

An cane fields unkept an dry.
Export a carry de swing.

Export de valuable tings,
Brother more serious wid brother,
Money talk,
Bullshit walk.
An Beverly Hills,
Jus a nassie up de area,
Wid dem new ranger rover,
Dat de American bring,
An string of other poisionous things.

© Nefertiti Gayle

Agitated

Agitated Black woman,
Agitated my friend,
What is happening,
With African men?

Some inna prison,
Some on Cocaine,
Some wid European women.

Agitated Black daughter,
Agitated children,
A break-down,
Of our family system.

Som say Black woman,
Agitated,
While some look at dem,
Underrated,
Some want to be,
The Black woman mouth piece,
But they can never,
Sit in her seat.

She wok so hard,
For her African youth,
Even though Babylon,
Is a brute,

She knows her children,
Must know the truth.

Agitated Black families,
Agitated my friend,
African youth a walk street,
Wid dem friend,
An en up like robot,
Through government system,
Agitated through no patience,
Or love.
Agitation,
Penetration,
Bodderation,
Bad vibration,

Separation.

© Nefertiti Gayle

Escape

I've got to get out of here,
Got to be where I know myself.
I don't want to be near,
The hustle and the bustle,
I don't want to hear the cars,
Blaring their horns!
I want to hear the child,
Crying mummy, mummy, mummy.
I want to hear and see,
The writing on the wall.

It's such a pleasant space,
But I feel so out of place.
I can endure it for a while,
If I don't get that certain smile,
I may as well be in exile.

I don't want to be near,
The hustle and the bustle,
I don't want to hear the cars,
Blaring their horns!
Always be there children,
Crying mummy, mummy, mummy.
Playing in the streets,
Singing soft and sweet,
And people! Oh you know people!
From all walks of life.

44

Sharing in confusion,
Sharing in the strife,
Sharing in love,
Sharing in life.
Fighting all the hustle,
Fighting all the bustle,
Knowing all the ploys,
And feeling all the joys of life.

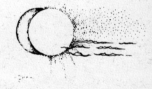

International Exploitation

International Exploitation!
The murder of a nation.
Cultural starvation.
False christianity,
Drives a nation to insanity.

The selling of souls,
To reinforce european strongholds!

International Exploitation!
The murder of a nation.
Cultural starvation.
False christianity,
Drives a nation to insanity.

Neocolonialism reigns supreme,
America implants her nuclear dreams,
People starve,
Too weak to fight back.
East West powers continual attack!

Supporting the grooming,
Of capitalist Blacks!

International Exploitation!
The murder of a nation.
Cultural starvation.
False christianity,
Drives a nation to insanity.

Economics of the stomach,
Enslavement of minds.
Propagation of family planning,
To advance genocide.
East West governments blame,
Natural elements,
For the destruction of lives,
But when the truth is spoken,
East West media dismiss it as lies!

International Exploitation!
The murder of a nation,
Cultural starvation,
False christianity,
Drives a nation to insanity.

Cash crops planted for export,
People starving,
Cause of the forces of greed and evil.
The destruction of a civilisation!
Has brought it to starvation!

International Exploitation!
The murder of a nation.
Cultural starvation.
False christianity,
Drives a nation to insanity.
The selling of souls,
To reinforce european strongholds!

© Fyna Dowe/Nefertiti Gayle

Raison d'être
(The Reason for Being)

They said the reason for being,
Is a question on a question,
Always search for the right direction.
Life is a circle which always reflects back,
People are complicated,
But become elementary on contact.
Hopes and dreams will always override,
Endeavours which once seemed
      too big a stride.
Personalities may differ,
Yet project a similar vibe.
Attitudes inconsistent,
Shielding a hidden side.
Yearning and learning,
To experience more,
Noting no one is indispensible,
So they said, evaluate, question,
Respect yourself,
And others who show it,
And the question and answer,
Will manifest itself,
Before you know it.

© Fyna Dowe 1984

Stan Firm

Stan firm,
African daughter,
Stan firm,
Inna dis ya time.
Everyone is trying to steal our minds.
An some only want our behinds.

© Nefertiti Gayle

I Am What I Am

I am what I am,
An no other image.
I am what I am,
Decended from my people.
I like what I am.
The colour of my skin,
The texture of my hair,
My facial structure,
My behind,
My large feet and course soles.
The rhythm in my hips,
The movement in my hand,
My behind.
I am what I am,
I am no other image.

© Nefertiti Gayle

Miscegenation

Miscegenation of the race
Is a very big thing.
Thats why the word is
So Lonnnnnnnnnnnnnng,
And the line is
So thin.

Fyne Dowe

I Wonder Why

I open my eyes and see the sun,
Beam down to the ground like
    clouds on the run.
Dust-mingling-beams locked in a storm,
The feeling it gives me is happy and warm.
Another day is here rushing by,
A moment of madness,
And I wonder why?

Because you were not there,
In the pain and the sadness.
It's always lurking there.
In these hours of madness.

Meaningless rhymes,
Nonsensical schemes,
Play on my mind and appear in my dreams.
Reality is distant its meaning unclear,
Fear fighting back with a vengance so true.
Because I was really there but where were you?

In the pain and the sadness,
I was there,
In that moment of madness,
I was there!
In the pain the sadness,
I was there.
In that moment of madness,
I was there.

^c Fyna Dowe 1983

Forwad Out De My African Daughters

Forwad out de,
My African daughters,
Forwad out de,
In dis time,
Forwad wid strength,
My African sister,
Forwad wid pride,
Black mother.

Stan firm,
Stan proud,
Stan wid out fear.

Don't bow don't bow,
Don't bow to no one.

Wipe off that paint,
Of mental enslavement,
Dash wey the Western mentality.
Be the bark of the tree,
Like you have always been,
To set your children,
Generation free.

Free from 400 years of captivity,
Free from genocide an atrocities,
Free from Western brutality,
Free to be free in a new life to come.
Freeness within an African mentality.

© Nefertiti Gayle

Awakening

Trouble seems so close,
Yet the land of my ancestors,
Is so far away,
What can I do?
Wake up!
And lift that veil from your eyes,
Go look see,
What they've been doing,
While we were sleeping,
Waiting for the sun to rise.
I said wake up!
And lift that veil from your eyes,
Go look see,
What they've been doing,
While we were sleeping,
Waiting for the sun to rise.

In the East there has been no peace,
Since that day turned to night,
Life surrendered to hell!
And we fell into a deep sleep,
Dreamed dreams,
We did not want to,
So this I say to you,
Wake up!
And lift that veil from your eyes,
Go look, Go look,

see what they've been doing,
While we were sleeping.
Waiting for the sun to rise.

Because the day will soon be here
When they will all fear,
Because the sun will set
And that sun will rise
And open wide your eyes.

Wake up! Wake up!
Wake up! Cos we've got to be free,
Wake up! Cos we've got to learn to see,
Wake up! Wake up!

And lift that veil,
Lift that veil from your eyes,
I said lift that veil from your eyes.

Go help your brother over there,
To let him know that you care!
Go help your sister too.
Because she needs you — Ah now

Wake them up!
You've got to wake them up!
And show them
Show us,
That the sun will rise!

Room At The Top

There is room at the top,
It cannot accommodate a lot,
So men say, what a price to pay,
Women are not allowed to penetrate,
The no go zone,
Their place is home, alone.
Oh No, No . . . No, No, No, No!

There is room at the top,
We cannot accommodate you all,
You are too tall, you are too small,
These excuses that they make!
Decide our fate!
You've got big ears,
Face full of tears,
Your colour is not right,
Eyes too bright.
Oh No, No . . . No, No, No, No! . . .

There is room at the top,
We will not accommodate you any more,
What ever for?
Because we are quite sure,
If we unlock the door of the zone,
It will break our backbone,
Then we'll fall like Rome,
Oh No, No . . . No, No, No, No!

There is room at the top!
There is room at the top!
There is room at the top!

Herpes

Coming from the musical quarters,
From the dreader African daughters,
Come to mash down Babylan quaters,
This is a message to all dem man,
Who walk around wid dem ego in dem han.
Herpes a spread like breeze,
Even start fe grow pon trees,
An it come out you nose when you sneeze,
Achoo!! Achoo!!
So keep away from some a dem daughters,
They are bound to bring you to be slaughter,
Cos Herpes a run like water.
Herpes a run like water.

Say de man dem a deal in slackness,
Dem a wallow, wallow, wallow in dem badness,
While de daughter ha fe deal with Blackness.
A wa you say!?
It's no time we deal wid our Africaness.
It no time we deal wid out Africaness.
Say de man is a cool operator,
An him come wid him big generator,
De woman is a big alligater,
Say de woman is a big alligater.
The alligater bite and de man tek a fright.
The alligater bite and de man tek a fright.

You should a see him run,
Till him tumble to de grun.
You should a see him run,
Till him ruble to de grun.

This is a message to all dem man,
Who walk around wid dem ego in dem han.
Herpes a spread like breeze,
Even start fe grow pon trees,
An it come out you nose when you sneeze,
Achoo!! Achoo!!

Lick dem wid de rod of correction!
BO!!
Kick dem in all direction!
BIFF!!
Daughters always giving protection,
An end up ina different direction.
De Black race don't need no infection,
De Black race don't need no infection.

Warn dem, tell dem, teach dem,
Warn dem, tell dem, teach dem,
Warn dem, tell dem, teach dem,

WARN DEM!!!

Reggae War

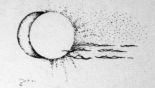

We must control our music,
We must control our land
Reggae music a we own,
Not David Rob-An-Gone.

Mash it up Rob An Gone mash it up!
Paper radio,
Rob An Gone reggae show.

Rob An Gone is a bobylan!
We don't check for that man.

Him put together a little reggae show,
An now him want control we dough.
Him patronise all the reggae artists,
Think him is the boss at it.

Rob An Gone is a bobylan,
We don't check for that man.

Some African people listen to that show,
And start saying Rob An Gone at the control!
Dem think it's really cool,
But dem no know Rob An Gone
        a turn dem fool.

Rob An Gone is a bobylan,
We don't check for that man.
Rob An Gone is a bobylan,
We don't check for that man.

African D.J. play D.J. must play!
African D.J. play
African D.J. play
Reggae music,
Soul music,
Jazz music,
Calypso music,
African music.
Him go investigate our reggae music,
Him go down into Black man lan!
Gone down with his plan,
To thieve information out of Black man han.

Go away Rob An Gone go way!
Is what you think you know?
We African people are fed up,
Of de little bogus show,
At paper radio.

South Africa trades with your country,
Giving your programme nuff money,
We African people don't find it funny,
When our people are still no free.

Rob An Gone is a bobylan,
We don't check for that man!

You think you have we in you han,
But one thing you must understan,
You'll always be a bobylan!

Go away Rob An Gone go way!
No act as expert fe we,
No act as spokesman fe we,
Cos we don't need you in we family.

Fyna Dowe/Nefertiti Gayle

African People Time

African people time we hav fe check,
We mind,
African people time, we hav fe check,
We mind.
Some wid M.16 already on de scene,
Nuclear bomb coming on strong.
Some can't pay the rent, dem a jump fence.
Gun man come inna tennament yard,
Thinking him is really hard,
You life get threaten everyday,
No matter where de rent fe pay.

Sister abused, man confused.
Sister abused, dem tan up strong
Some man think de daughters wrong,
To have an independent life,
Instead of being a beaten wife
Neglected children running wild
Developing Western style.
No African teaching,
Only Western preaching.

African people time we hav fe check
We mind
African people time, we hav fe check
We mind.

66

Intergration as a token gesture,
While mental enslavement continues
To fester.
Falling in love is not the answer,
To explain away a multiracial disaster.

Love can only come after,
When races develop
Respect for each and everyone,
No matter where they come from.
Until we arrive at this conclusion.

We must not be deluded,
About where the power structure lies,
African people must control their own lives,
And not be blinded by Western lies,
In disguise.

It's African people time,
We hav fe check out we mind,
Only positive African vibes,
No Western disguise,
No Western lies.

Only positive African vibes,
No Western disguise,
Positive,
Positive,
Positive.

Your time,
My time,
Our time,

African people time . . .

67

Tiro Ese Emisiwe
Ka Sepe
(Nothing Must Stop the Work)

Some say the only reason for famine,
Is drought.
But I can show you things that will,
Cancel this lie right out.

Tiro Ese Emisiwe Ka Sepe,
Nothing must stop the work.
Tiro Ese Emisiwe Ka Sepe,
Nothing must stop the work.

The work deals with our minds.
It is not to be romaticised!

Take time to know our history,
There you'll find the reasons why,
We must be free.

Some are frightened of their minds,
Hide behind fantacies,
Material wealth.
They need not be afraid,
Because this fear,
Is only man made.

I say Tiro Ese Emisiwe Ka Sepe,
Nothing must stop the work.
Nothing — No!
Nothing will stop the work.

Don't say "there isn't anything"
    you can do,
Or you "have tried".

My message to you is,
"Get wise".

Wise up to capital lies,
War economics.
What is made on life,
Is a murderous profit,
It's murder, murder, murder, murder.

Know: why governments want to keep
    the people poor.
And puppet heads of states are always,
Begging for more.
Begging, Begging, Begging, Begging,
Begging for more!

Know why they keep our history back.
And denounce anything Black.
Check the so called politics of the free
Who preach justice and democracy.
But, commit genocide and
Create wars, they create, create create wars
It should not be so.

Tiro Ese Emisiwe Ka Sepe,
Means getting the family together.
Realising who we are,
When we achieve this aim.
We will realise
We will relise the struggle is not in vain
        The struggle is not in vain.

What Will You Do?

You sit inside your cover,
Only to discover.
Many inconsistances.
Many overt mysteries.

What do you think?
What can you say?

When one is white as night,
And one is Black as day!
Seeing the children in confusion,
Full of disillusion,
What will you do?

Locked in your fabricated world.
Hiding from reality.
You think you have gone too far,
To face reality.

What do you think?
What can you say?

When one is white as night!
And one is Black as day!

Your child's mind,
Respect has slipped away.

Woman, Man
You say you have tried so hard
     to make a stand.
It always ends the same,
The inevitable broken chain.
I see you sit and wonder,
Is it too late?
To regain,
Your mental state?
Your self,
Your name?

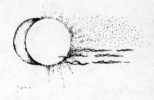

Nigerian Occupation

Nigerian occupation,
Infection of a nation.
Spending your time,
Following the capital carrot,
Speaking like a trained parrot.
Corrupt,
Within your egoist self,
Engulfed,
In your dishonestly earned wealth.

Arrogant,
Boastful,
Selfish,
Bad!
Women
Treated as objects of perversion,
Travelling
A road of which you are uncertain,
Nira controller,
Woman cajoler!

Nigerian occupation
Infection of a nation.

Omm . . . Shame, Shame,
Shame, Shame, Shame!
Look! How we a follow money,

All the time,
Our mind is on money,
Do, Do, Do,
Do, DO, Do,
How our minds gone bad!
Listen to me people!
People understand me,
We are doing it all wrong.

Left, right-not even democratic,
Over all our beliefs momentarily estatic,
Caught in the rat race,
Putting on a face,
Trying,
To gain an accepted place.

You,
Who profess to be so cultured,
Behave even worse than the vultures,
Outside educated,

Mind totally disorientated!!
Nigerian occupation,
Infection of a nation!

© Fyna Dowe 1981

Sally & Harry

Sally was a virigo gal,
An Harry was da gorgon.
Sally do six years bird,
Harry! him stay outside an work,
Work get car,
Get some gold,
Get some chick's
O boy him rich.

Sally do cheques give Harry,
Is through dat,
Him an her marry,
But remember,
Sally a virigo gal.

Sally finish do bird,
Harry three piece suit an ting,
Big house, car, chick,
Sally a look fe Harry.

She tred down a Finsbury Park,
Pass all da boys in chamber,
Out a da bookie shop.
WAAHAPN Sally,
We Harry,
Sally just cut her eye,
And just bob.

She stride pass,
Roy barber shop,
WAAHAPN gal,
Me no cut ya hair last week,
Wa ya do walk street,
Sally just cut her eye and just bob.

When she reach,
We she have to reach,
She stan up still,
Boy bottle a go mash,
She go knock at da door,
Da sister come out,
Harry bawl out,
Sally da sister a carry.
Sally pull,
Harry fall,
Sister bawl end of all.

© Nefertiti Gayle

How Does It Feel?

How does it feel:
Living in a world full of dreams?
Knowing everyday love,
And life has gone astray!
Tell me! How does it feel,
Living in a world full of schemes?
Seeing everyday,
Back-biting does not pay!

They will never lift you up,
They love it when you drop,
and some say,
There is a price to pay!

Always crying tears,
–face full of fear–
Your tunes not right,
Mind too bright!
It's no joke,
Where there is rain,
There is always hope,
It's no joke,
No matter what the price,
You'll always cope.

They will never lift you up!
They love it when you drop!
And some say there is a price to pay!

They will never lift you up!
They love it when you drop!
And some say there is a price to pay!

Sister Lou

Sister Lou,
Sister Lou,
Sister Lou,
She feel,
Well blue.

Leroy come,
Wid him two long han,
Out playing dominoes,
All night long,
Rent fe pay inna de yard,
Leroy spen' out him money,
Pon card!

Sister Lou,
She look well vex,
Leroy shame,
An start mek treats.
She pick a bottle,
An a jump an prance,
Leroy shame,
An start cus ras.

Han on kimbow,
Mout push out,
Sister Lou,
Give Leroy a clout.

Sister Lou,
What you do?
Leroy start,
To run after you!
Sister Lou,
Na feel blue,
She only did,
What she had to do.

Leroy get a lick,
An it serve him right,
Spen off him money,
An neglet him wife.

Leroy get a lick,
An it serve him right,
Spen off him money,
An neglet him wife.

Shame on you,
Shame on you,
Shame on you,
Now Leroy blue.

Straighten Hed Gal

Straighten hed gal,
Straighten hed gal,
Why yeh bun up,
Yeh hed fa gal.

Weave on gal,
Weave on gal,
What yeh a weave on,
Weave on gal.

Perm hed gal,
Perm hed gal,
Why you creame dat hed fa gal,

Wig gal,
Wig gal,
Why you wear dat wig fa gal,

Natural gal,
Natural gal,
Natural gal,
Is a African gal.

Fire

If you play with fire you will get burnt,
If you play with fire you will eventually learn.
Fire, Fire, Fire!
Fire, Fire, Fire!

Ammunition sounding from musicians,
Ammunition sounding in tradition.

Fire, Fire, Fire!

The world is filled with fire
Beneath subterranean seas,
The world is filled with fire
blowing in the breeze.

Fire, Fire, Fire!

People rally round in total confusion!
People rally round in total disillusion!
People rally round: To them there
      is no solution!
But, Fire, Fire, Fire! . . . Fire!!!

© Fyna Dowe 1983

Black Gal

Black gal,
Wa mek you tan so,
Black gal,
Wid di plait up head.
Black gal,
Weh you man de,
When you can't feed,
Di six pickney dem.

Gal how yo hand so rough,
How you hand so crough
Wa mek you walk off,
Di shoes heel dem,
Gal wa mek you tupid,
Dat you can't teach,
Di pickney dem.

Gal wa you man gi you,
When him garn to breed again,
Gal wa you wan do you,
Mek you beat di pickney dem,
Mek you walk da street dem.

Black gal,
No walk da street again,
No beat da pickney dem,
No fret bout man again,
Jus teach you pickney dem.

© Nefertiti Gayle

Inter — Racial

Inter Racial,
Multi racial,
Inter racial stuff.
What a mix up,
It's a mix up,
Mus deh be a mix up mus?

What about we?
We talk about unity,
And we jus a fight for
White man identity;
An forget about tradition an culture.

We brainwash,
We want to keep whitewash,
An integrated at a multi rate,
An have a inner racial stuff.

Inter racial
Multi racial,
Inter racial stuff.
What a mix up,
It's a mix up,
Mus deh a mix up mus?

But African man mek no plan,
Some don't even know bout dem lan,
Some don't count dem self as Black man.
An Black woman on de oder han,
Don't see dem self as no African.
All dem see is.

Inter racial,
Multi racial,
Inter racial stuff.
What a mix up,
It's a mix up,
Mus deh be a mix up mus?

So what about dem youths,
Who don't know de truth,
An dem is de seed,
Of a next generation,
An Mankind,
De seeds of de time,
Carry on blind,
Contaminating de situation,
An producing a more diluted,
African nation.

An de integrated seed,
Start to feed on
Dividing a nation.

Divide an rule,
Is de tool,
For destroying,
De Black man,
An Black woman relation,
Which in turn stop production,
Of a Black population.

Inter racial,
Multi racial,
Inter racial stuff,
What a mix up,
It's a mix up,
Mus deh be a mix up mus?

An some call for religion,
Saying there's no difference.
A colour of a man skin,
Don't change his aims,
But rape has produce,
De horrible truth.
De confusion,
An de humanisation,
of de Black man brain.

Inter racial,
Multi racial,
Inter racial stuff.
What a mix up,
It's a mix up,
Mus deh be a mix up mus?

Africa has suffered,
An African loss of some
Of it's brothers and sisters.
Some don't know,
An some weren't shown,
De direction from which dey came.
Some carry on saying,
Dey have no African blood,
Instead they say,
They have a european god,
An are proud of dere,
European names.

Inter Racial,
Multi racial,
Inter Racial stuff.
What a mix up,
It's a mix up,
Mus deh be a mix up mus?

An now in 1983 where Africa,
Should be free,
South Africa unveil a plan,
To give voting rights,
To indian man,
Voting rights to coloured
        citizens of mix decent.
An Black man,
No voting rights for African,
Now de time has come to realize,
Dat de West still a sterilize,
While poverty an starvation arise
Many African youth dies.
Western government summarise,
Dey issue de bills,
De west kills de will,
An many African stan still,
While from inside,
Dey invent de multi racial pill.

Inter racial,
Multi racial,
Inter racial,
Multi ethnic,
Talk of rhetoric,
But yet still they kill,
An many African stan still.

© Nefertiti Gayle

Tougher Laws

Tougher laws.
Tougher laws.
Tougher laws ya.

Riot shields,
sub machines,
battered youth,
hide the truth,

Tougher laws ya.

Shoot your mother.
Shoot your father.
Shoot your brother.
Shoot your sister.

Tougher laws ya.

They are trained
And equiped
To use any
dirty tak ticks.

They have their
orders
They have come.
An their main
weapon
Is the gun.
Tougher laws ya.

The dutch
And their allies
Refelct this force
Running out of Africa
To change the course
Running to Europe
To reinforce
Tougher laws ya.

Nefertiti Gayle ©

Women Wid De Gun

Women wid de gun gun gun
Gun dat yu ansestors never did have
fighting for freedom
fighting for LAND
fighting wid you pickney
    Ina yu han

You walk de ground
dat is yours
pounding
grounding
sounding
fighting
to recapture land
fighting beside you man.

As you walk
de lan talk
take me I am yours
recapture me for sure
release me
So my soil can be enriched
To grow de plant
dat belong to it.

Women wid a gun
baby on her back
using a map
to fight

de oppressor
who has always possess her
she a free up her
family lan
she a free up
her family lan
she a free up
her family lan

© Nefertiti Gayle

Romantic Struggle

Are you in love wid a
    Romantic Struggle???

A Romantic Struggle na get you no where,
Self-Egoism an insecure fear.
A Romantic Struggle is say it by de book.
Revolutionary songs . . . an de poetic look.

A Romantic Struggle is putting
    up Afrikan signs . . .
Steppin on yo bredder
    for your own gole mine . . .

A Romantic Struggle is a black leadership,
Leadin de way forward wid a European mix.
Multi-Racial society wid de
    white workers plight
National Front white workers delight
A Romantic Struggle is de Rastama
De commercialisation of de Rastaman
Exploitation of Selassie I
De use of Cally control by de big guy.
De trade of ganga for de M.16.
Brodder killin brodder.
Projection of de Western Scene.

A Romantic Struggle is de bourgeois black.
Wearin gerry curl an extension plait.
Wrappin up dey hed wid de Afrikan cloth.
Sittin down an chattin fart.
Settin up some false pipe dream
In-tel-lec-tua-lism on de
     mul-ti-ethnic scene.
Inviting Europeans to Afrikan Liberation Day.
An chantin songs of . . .
Blacks Are Here To Stay . . .
No Way No Way

A romantic struggle is de
Cultural trip
Talkin for de youts an
Segregatin dem from it.
Saying you're a brodder wid a conscious mind.
Fuckin up de daughter an
Leavin her behin.
Are you in Love wid a
Romantic Struggle . . .

A Letter From A Tired African Woman

Hail Jah Man,

I've been waiting around for you to come, siting up in bed loansome downsome no kiss or cuddles just another African man troubles over worked tired agitated getting faded love, promised by phone.

Nagging woman moves for more positive direction in her life. I've experience this before. I cannot be making the same mistake no more oh no! Emotional woman, can some times be blinded waddling in love, a European love with red hearts and bunches of flowers which has nothing to do with African struggle or shared love of one community one unity, but woman has to be forwad and disciplined traditional disciplin, not sitting around waiting for African mans love to unfold or even appears as gold. Independent woman needs her space but also needs her taste of sexual pleasures and supple measures this is natural this is nature, sometimes adds to inner strength.

African woman cannot keep getting blows playing with a woman feeling to frows and expecting her to understand mans troubles and worries when you have taken advantage and under estimate her mental ability to be a force to be recon with, waiting I cannot wait my patients won't permit me you have to be committed now not necessarily by vowe but been man caring for your family, having time to communicate else relationships deteriorate and you woman might masterbate or participate with another mate which then turns your feelings into dreadful hate, unable to trust or relate.

Woman needs time, time to share time to talk and widen our scope for a longer life with laughters and jokes. However Jah man lets face reality communication is the key giving you life to self awareness is not giving you life to me it can only strengthen we.

Nefertiti Gayle [©]